Faces

From The

Land

Drawings by

Drew Cottril

For Natalie, the love of my life.

A publication from

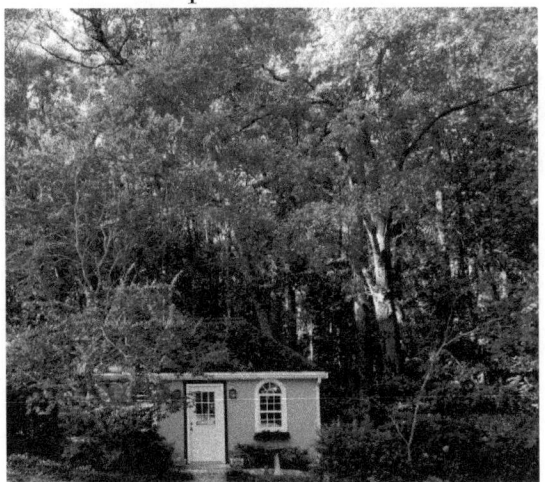

The Little Studio in the Woods

Faces from the Land

There are few things more interesting than the human face.

My subjects are people tied to the land as were their forefathers, who founded this great country. They are farmers, lumbermen, orchard men; they are kinsmen to all who worked the land before.

Their faces show the subtle humanity of God fearing, independent, hardworking souls whose images reflect their heritage of family and the land they work.

Some of the drawings are of faces from the past, others are contemporary and both are tied to the land.

Drew Cottril

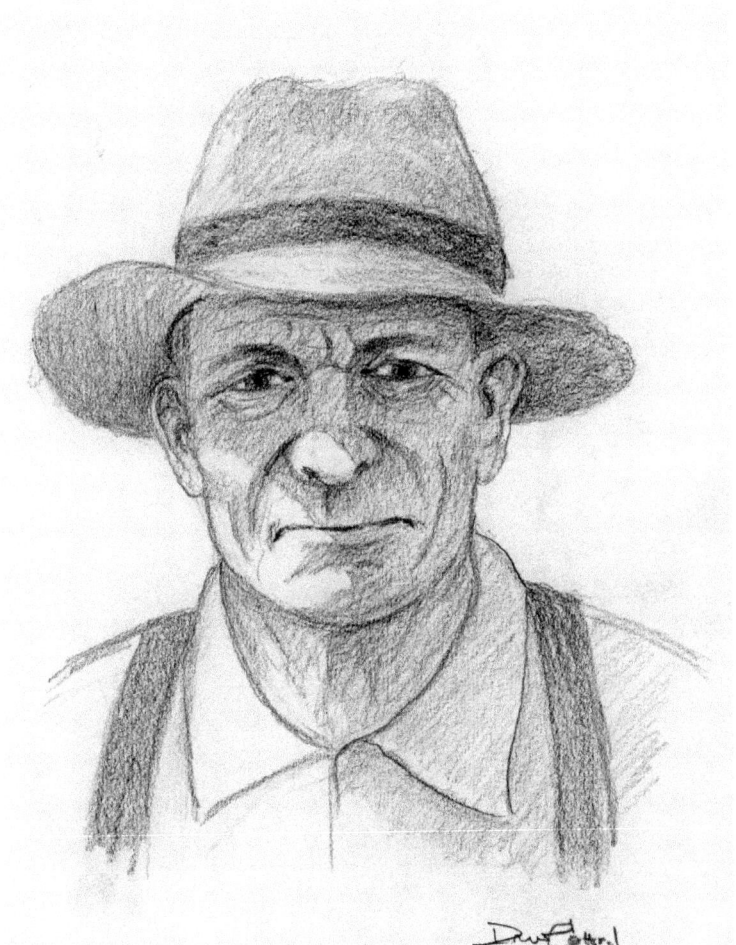

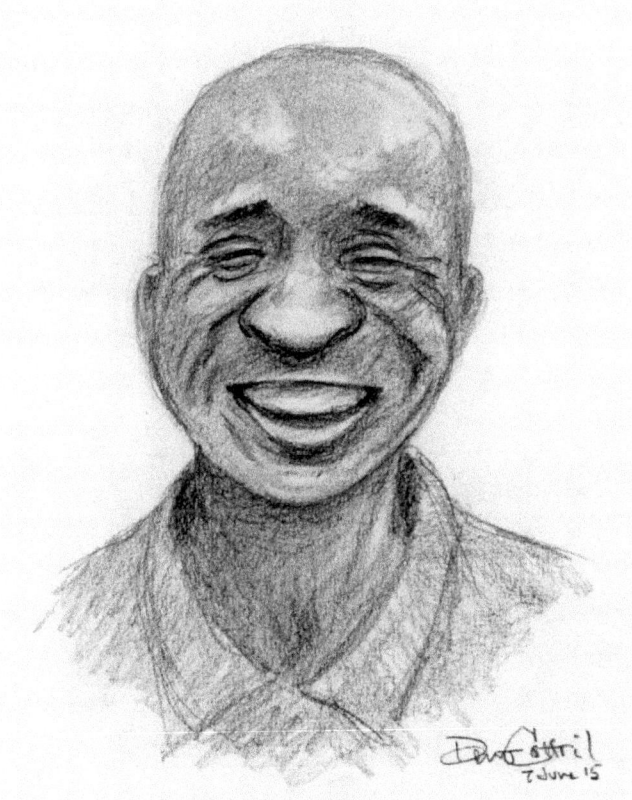

Dave Cottrill
7 June '15

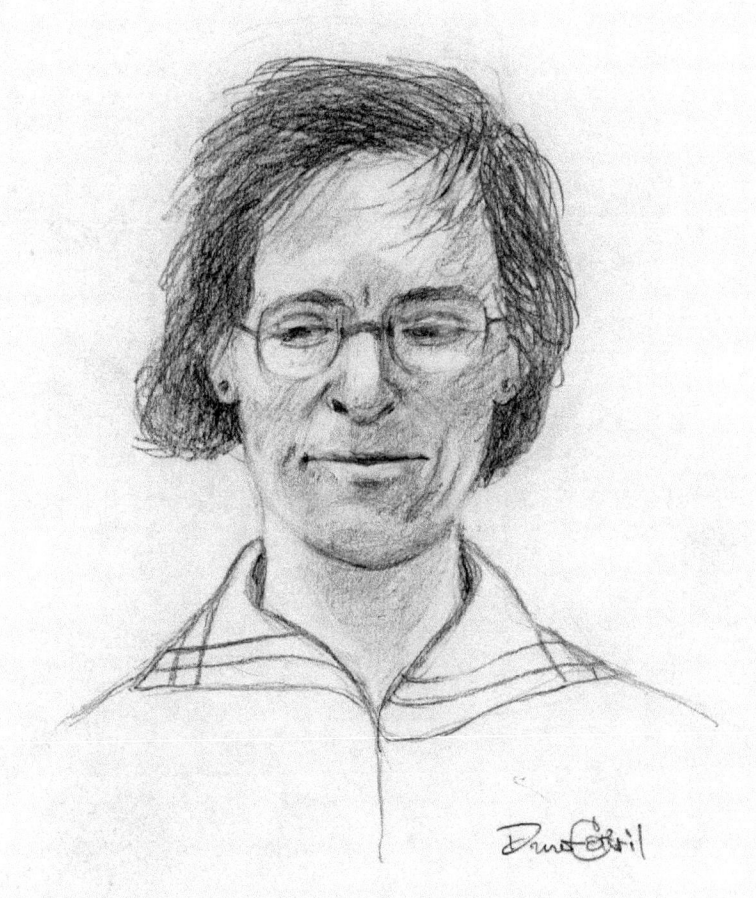

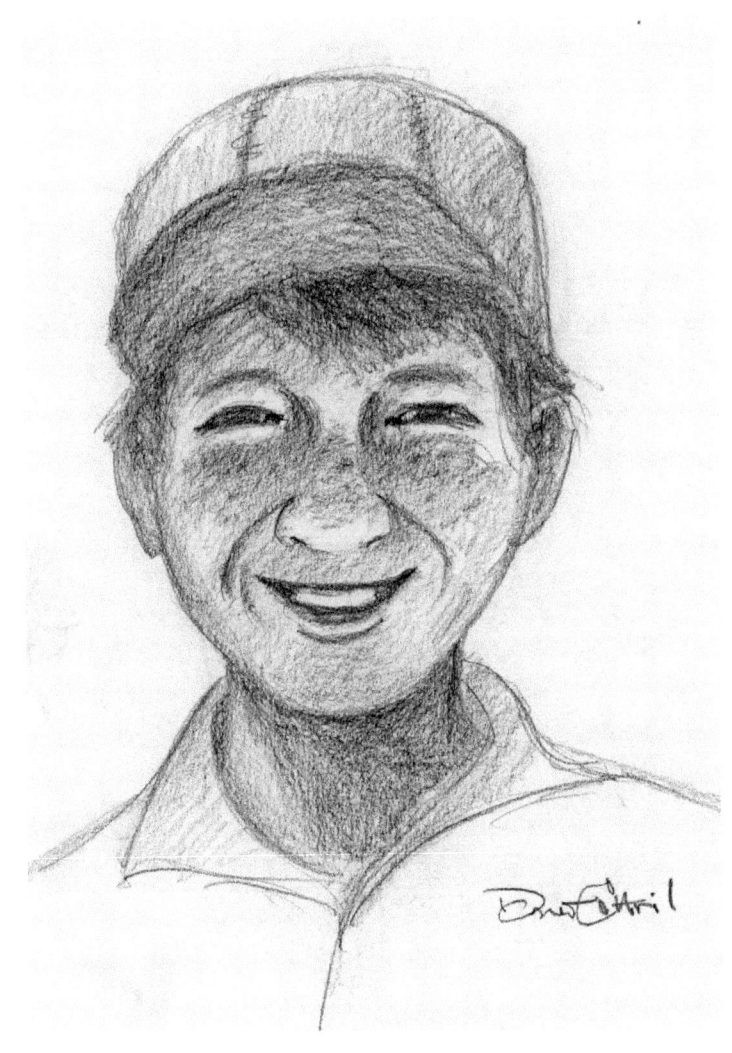

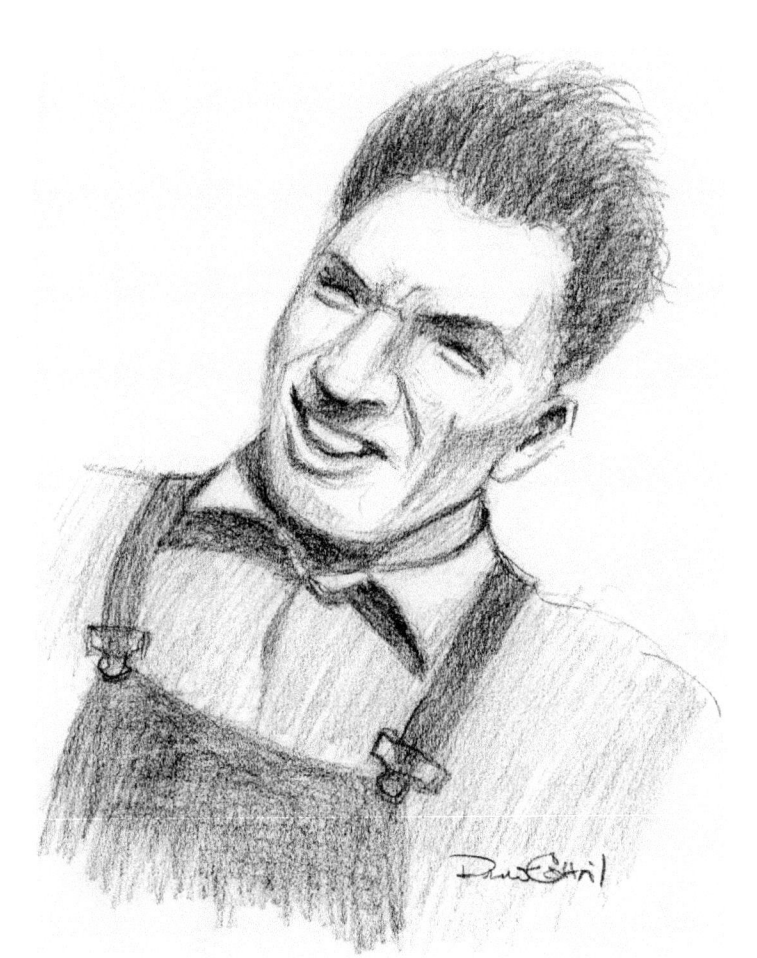

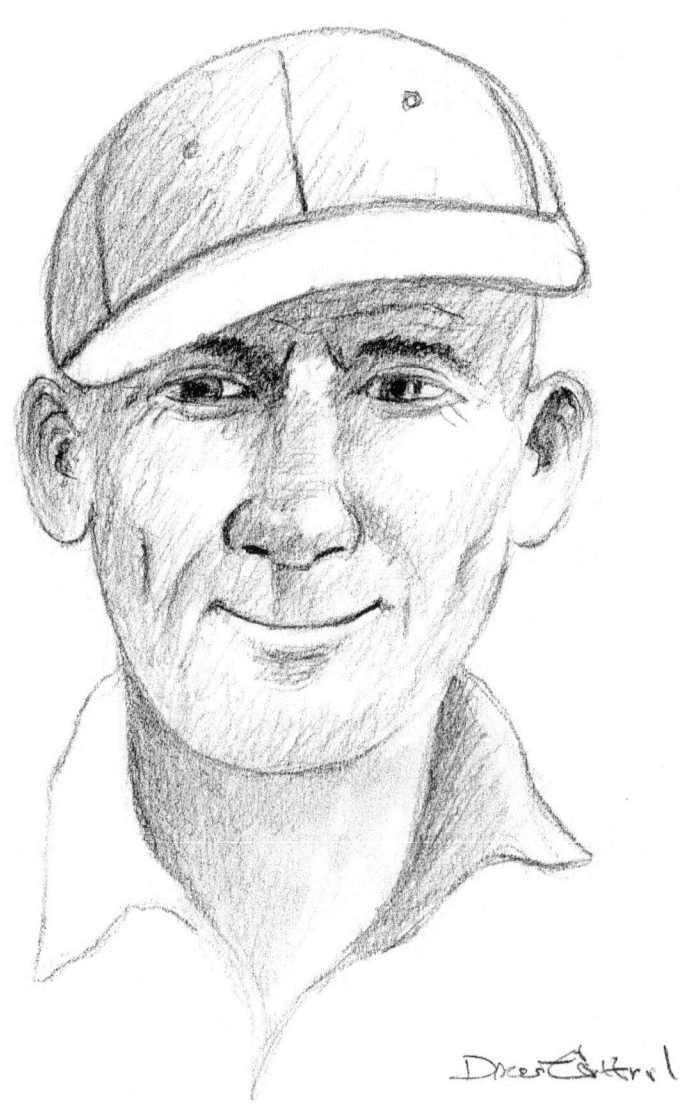

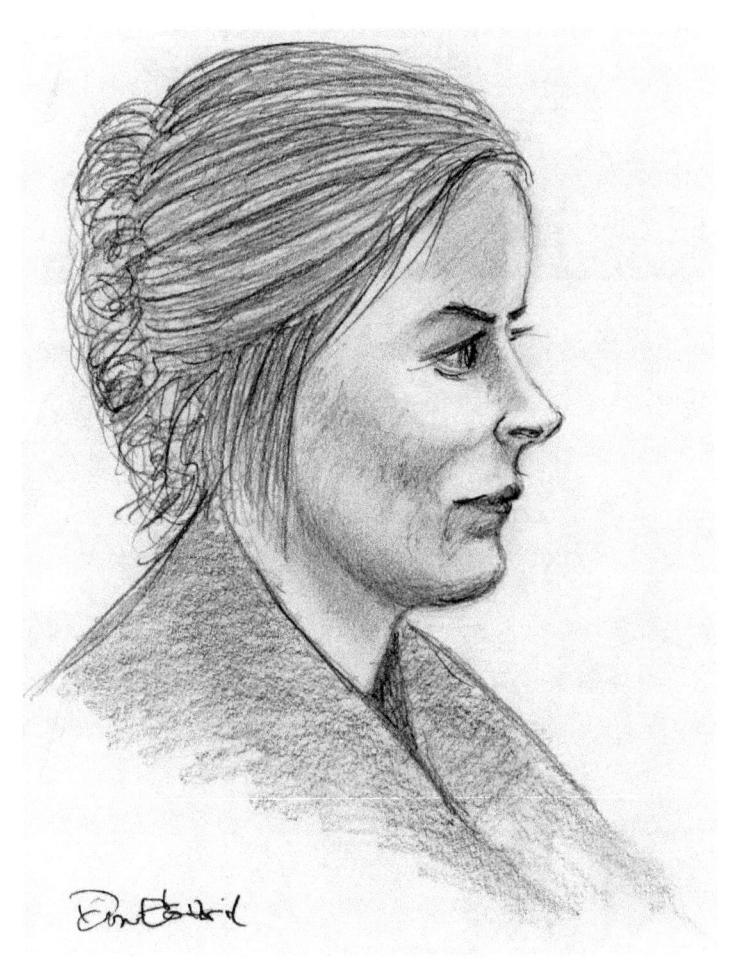

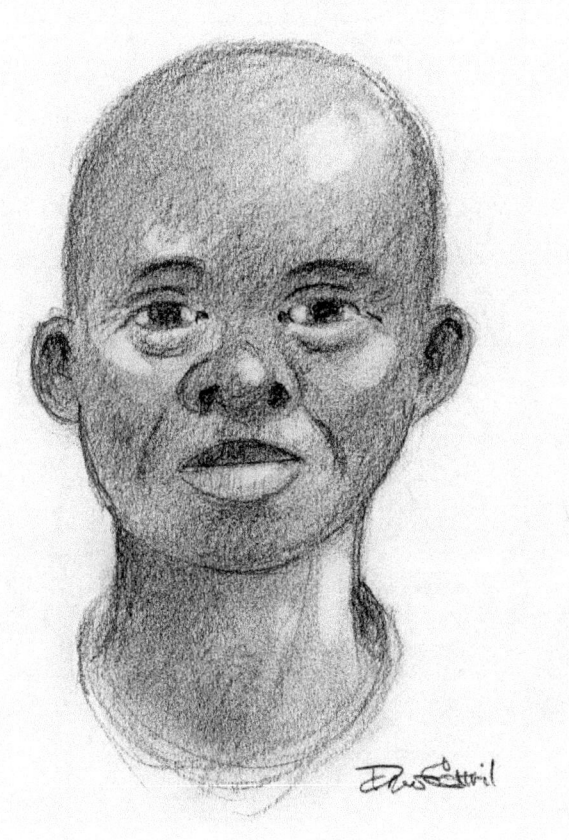

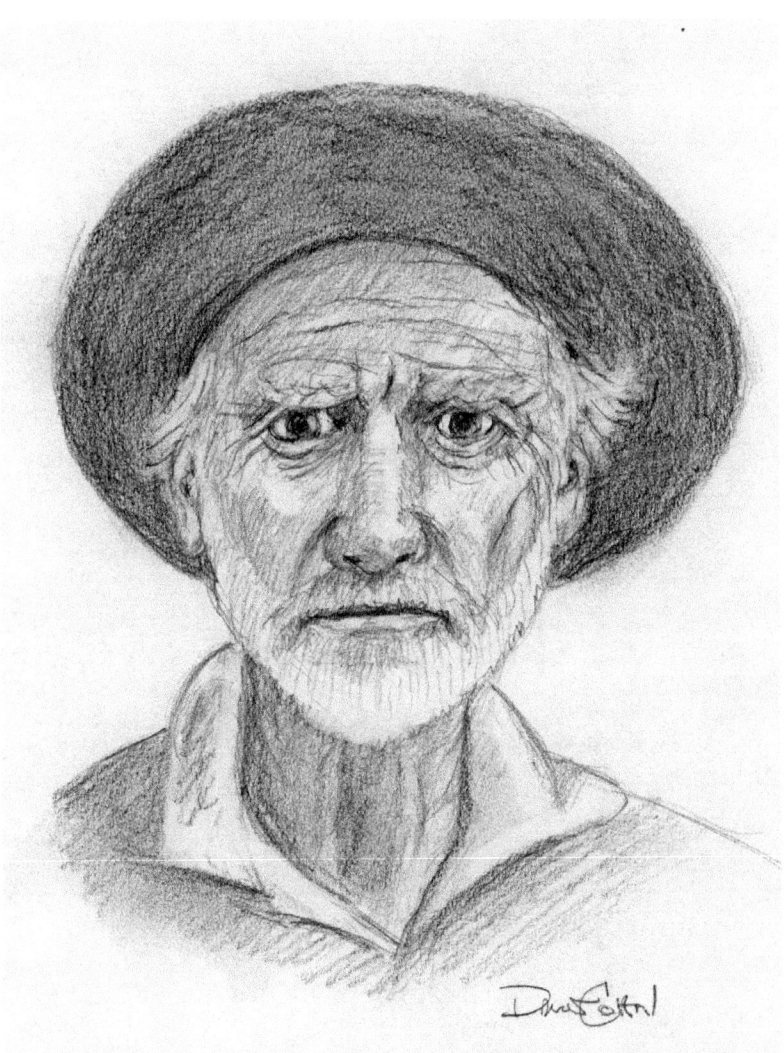

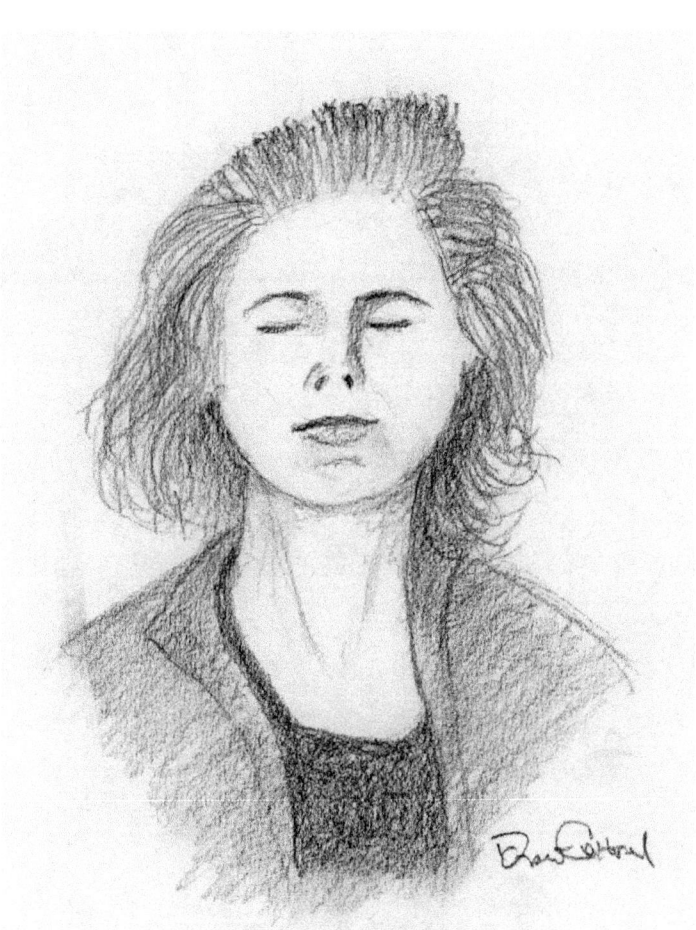

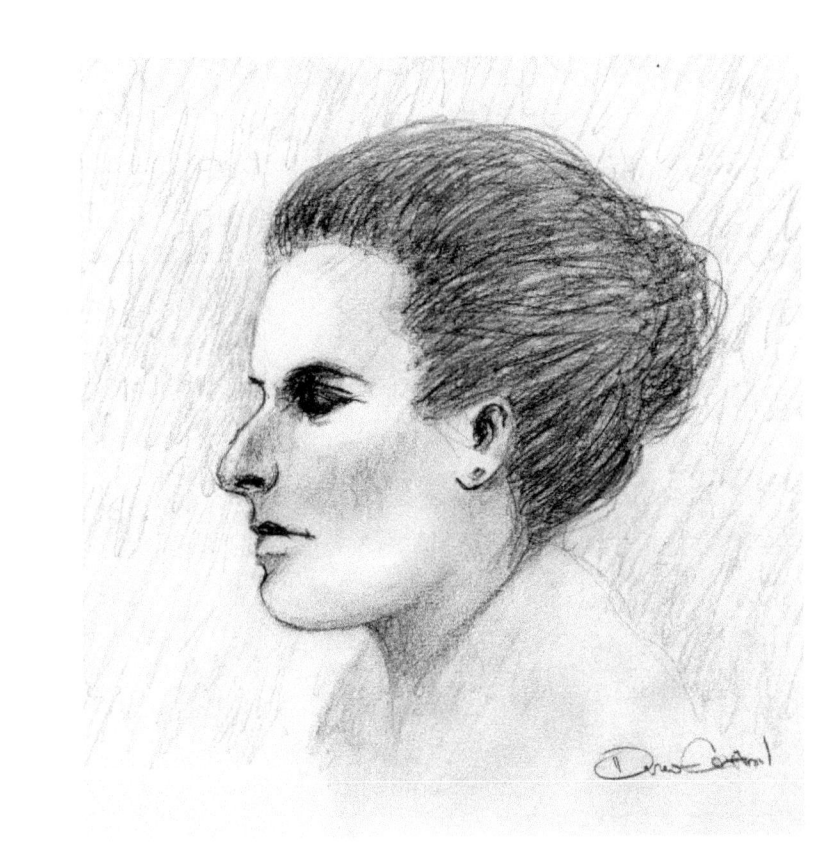

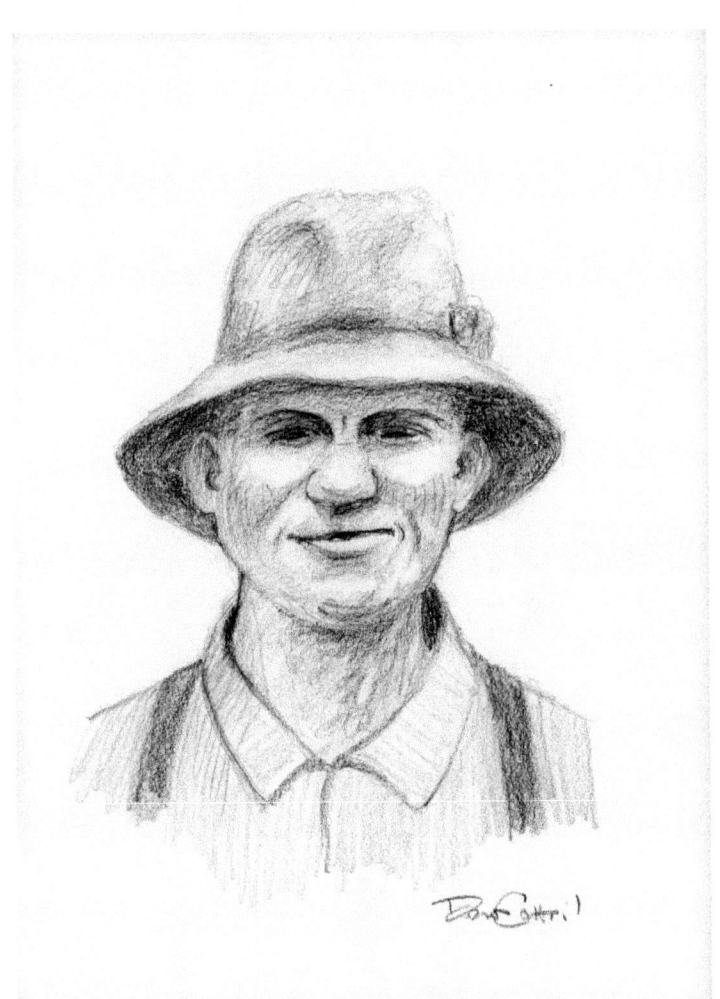

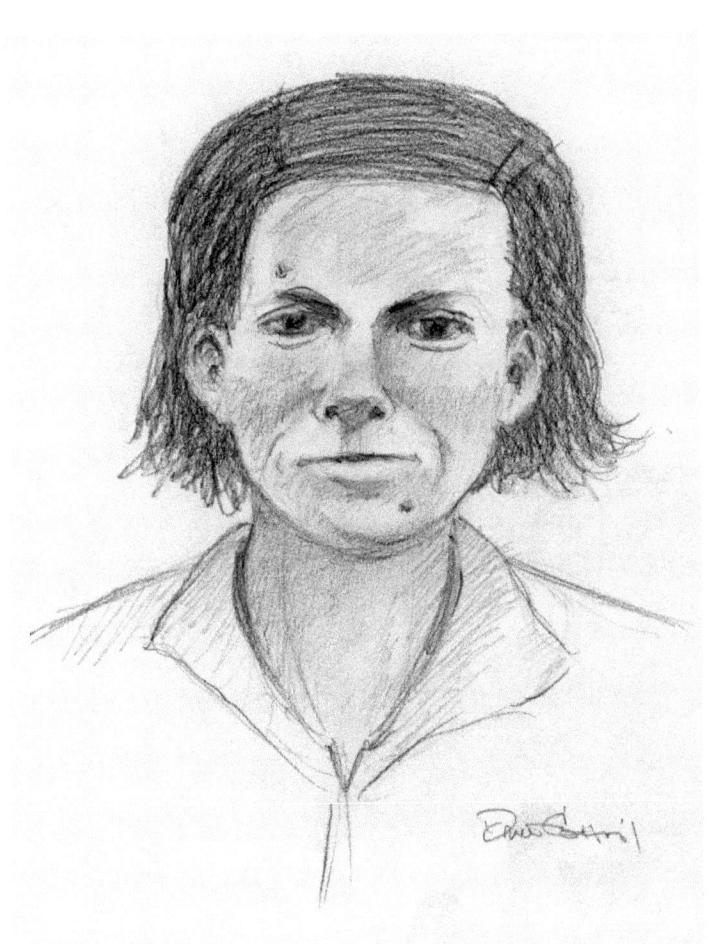

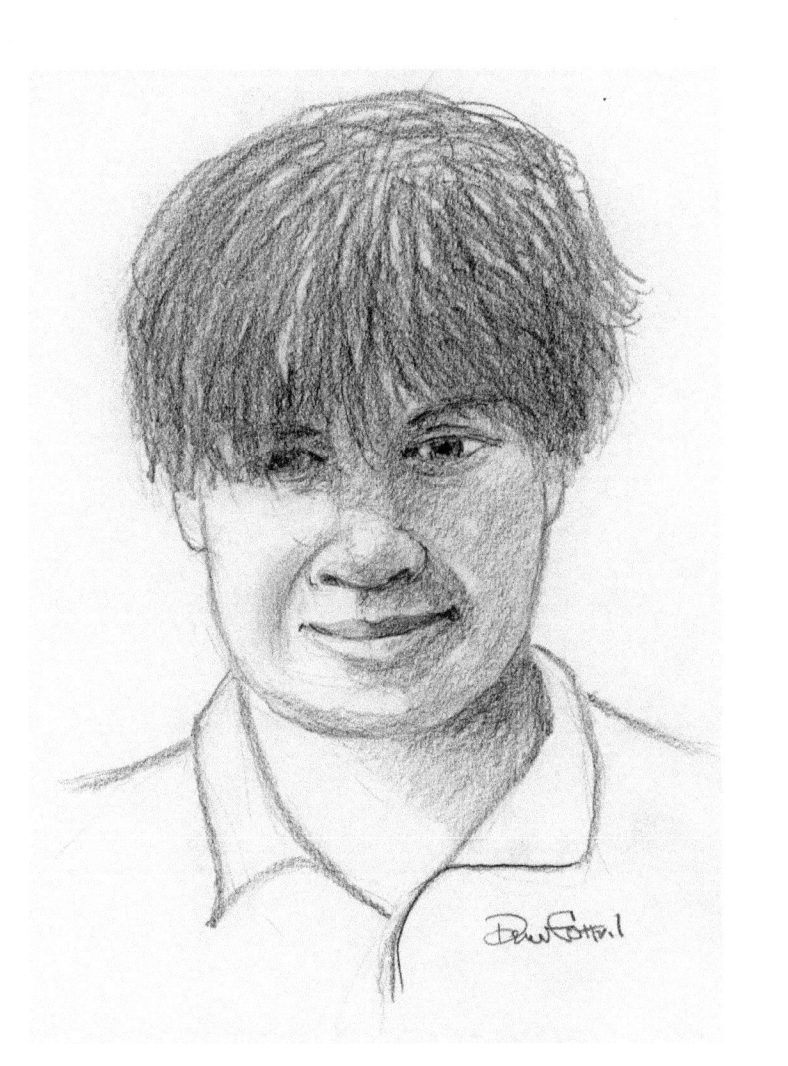

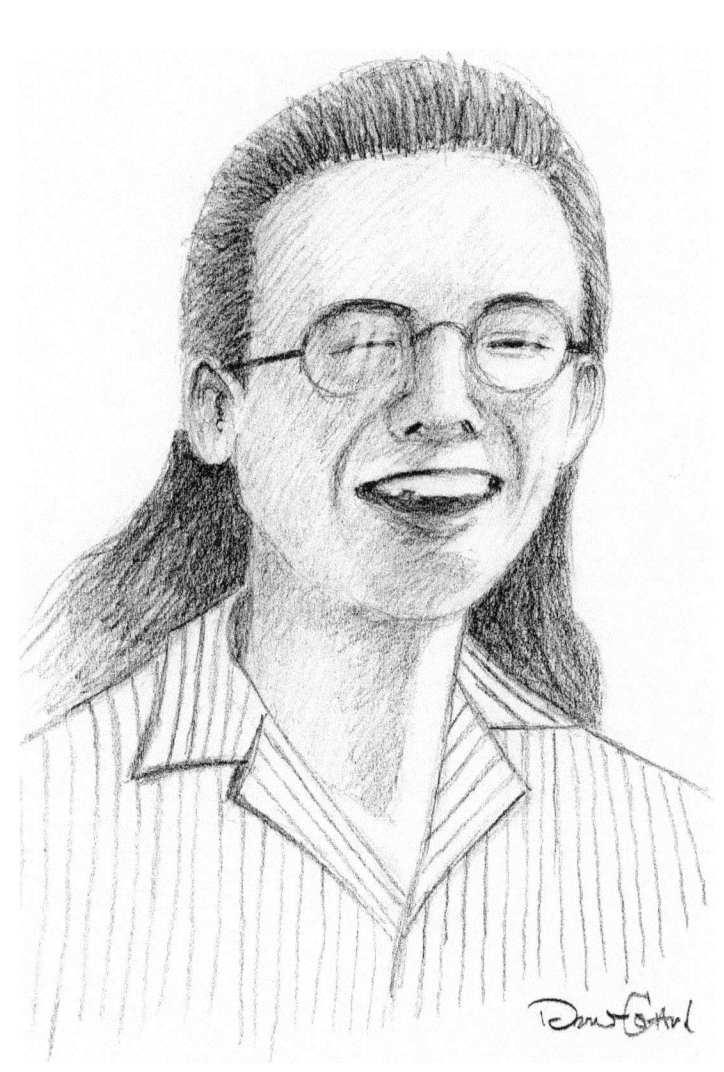

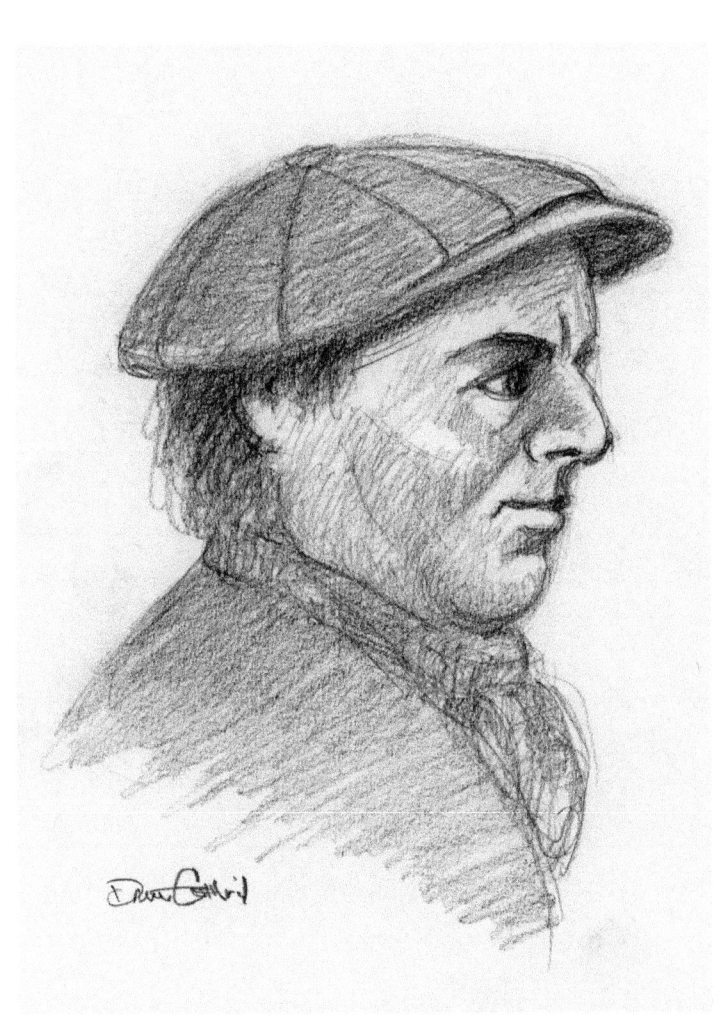

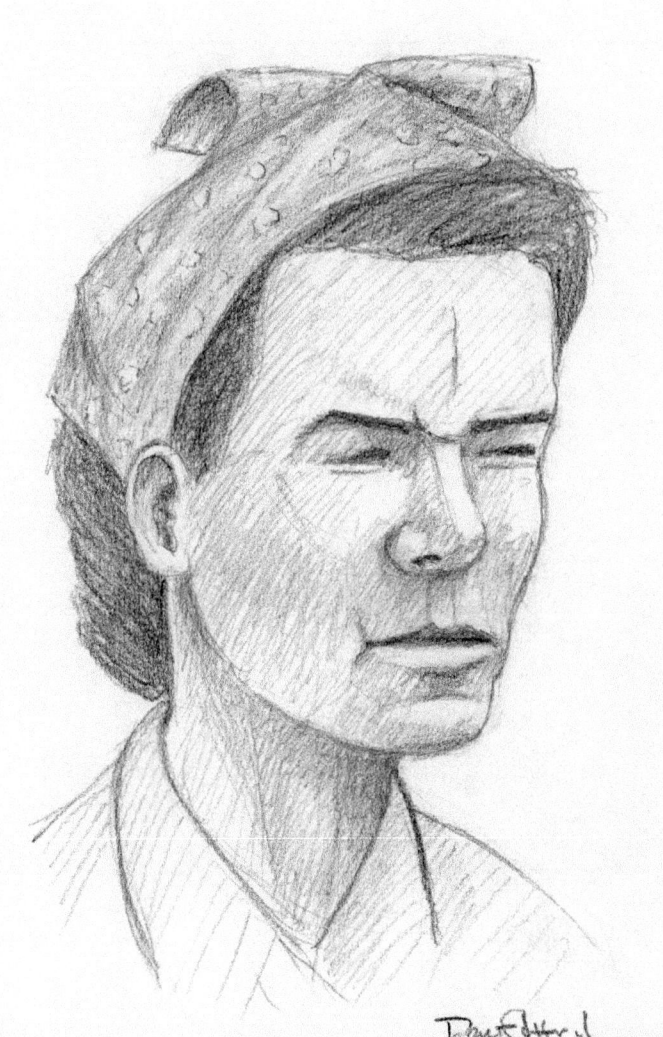

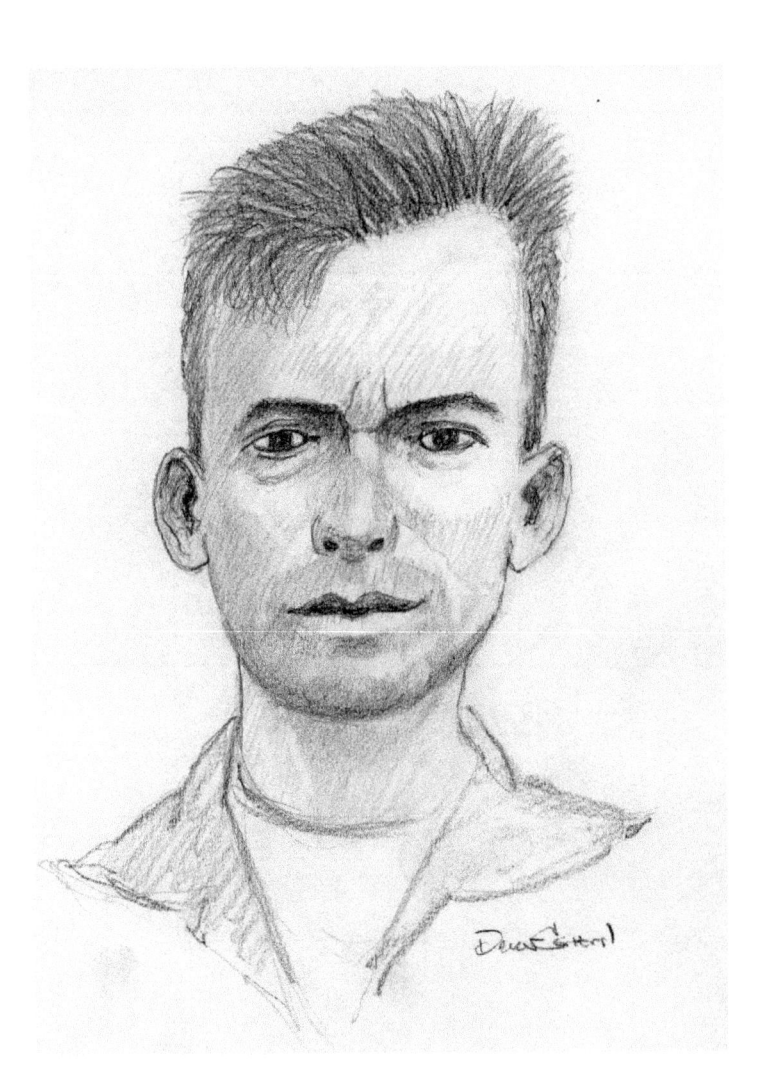

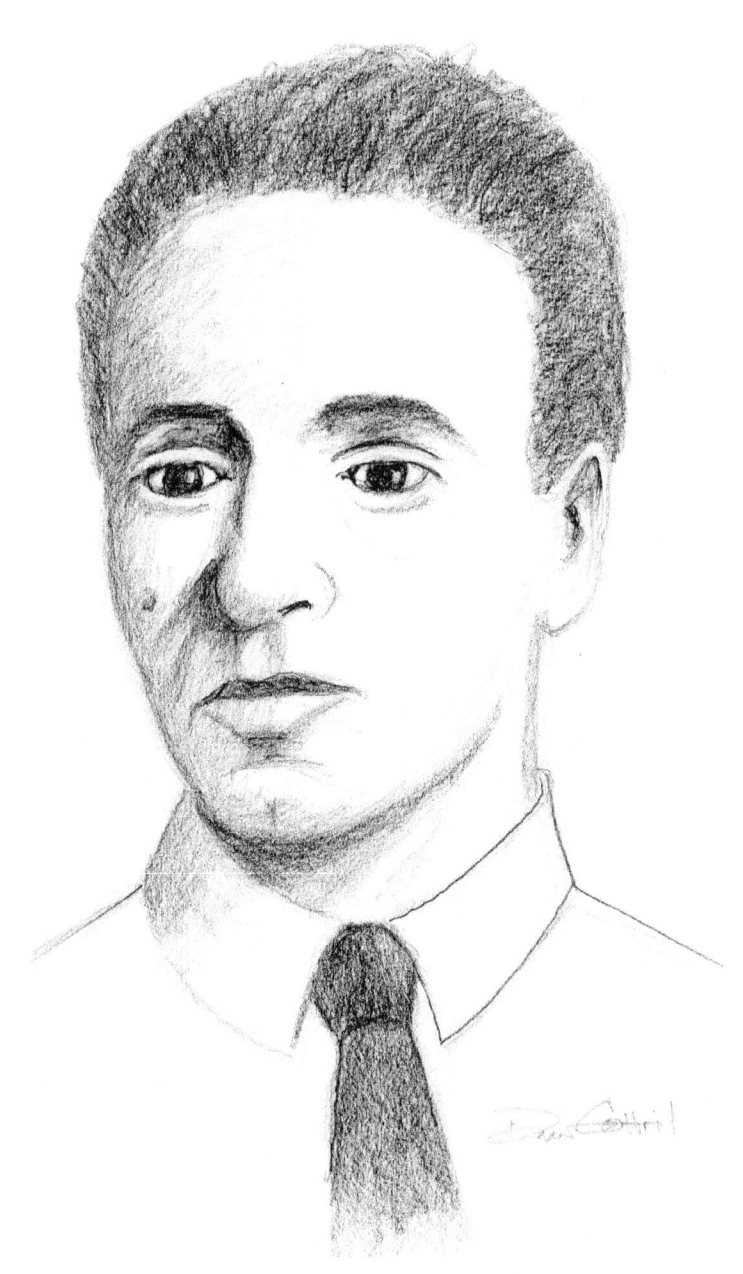

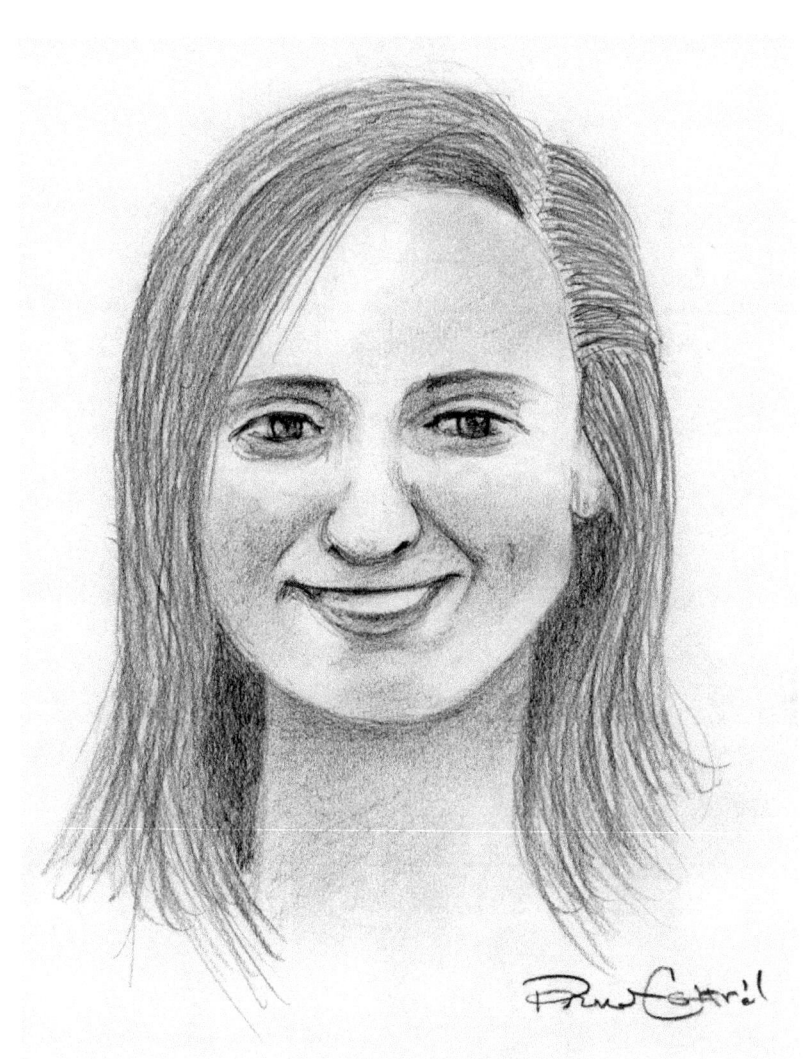

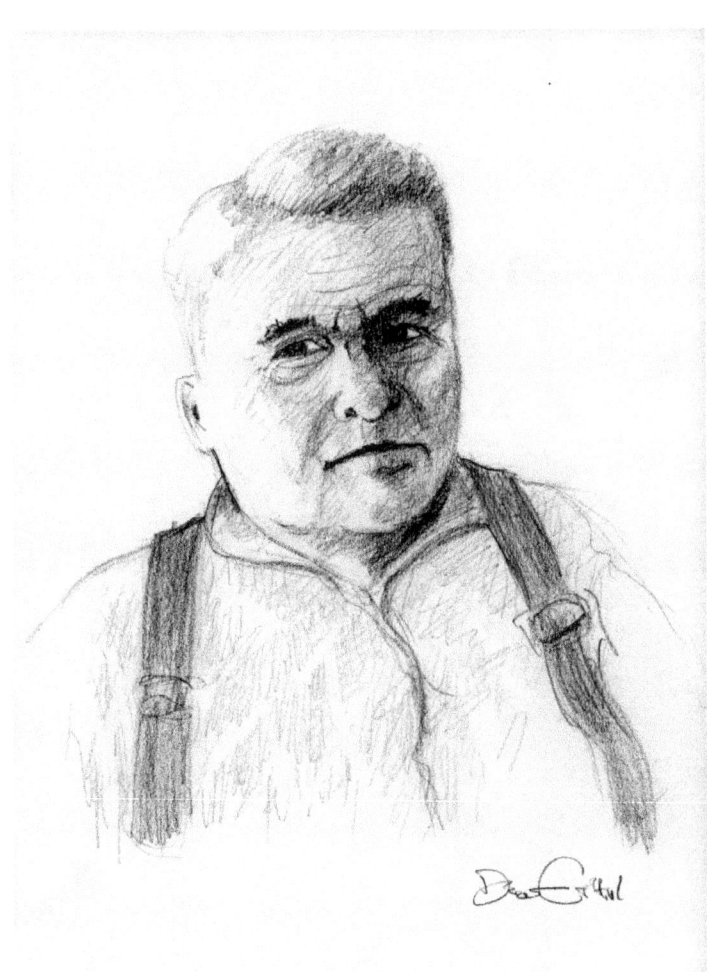

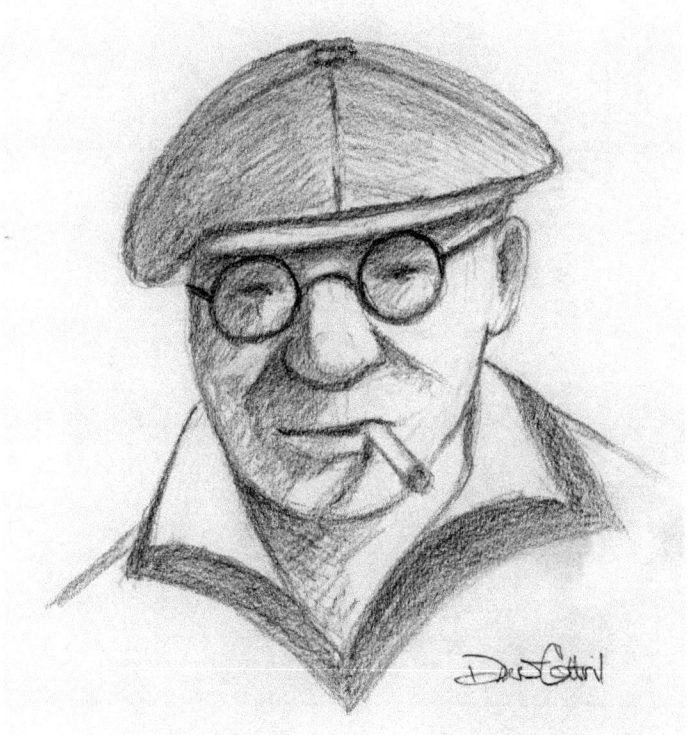

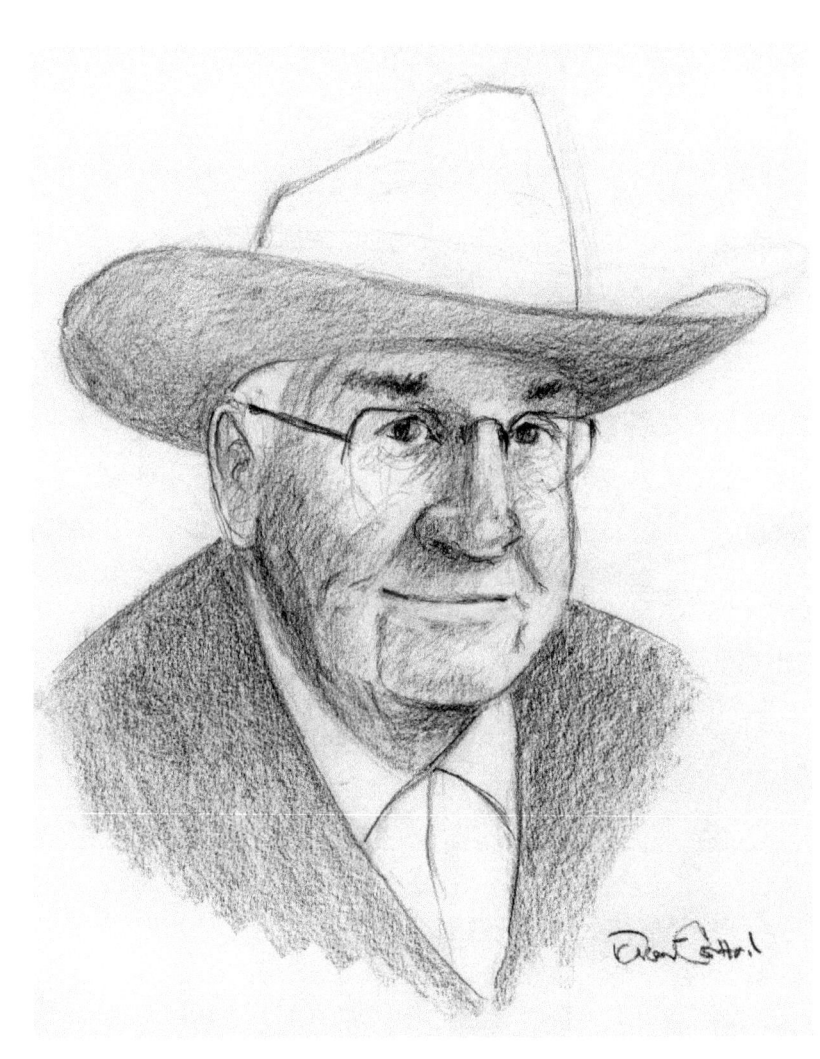

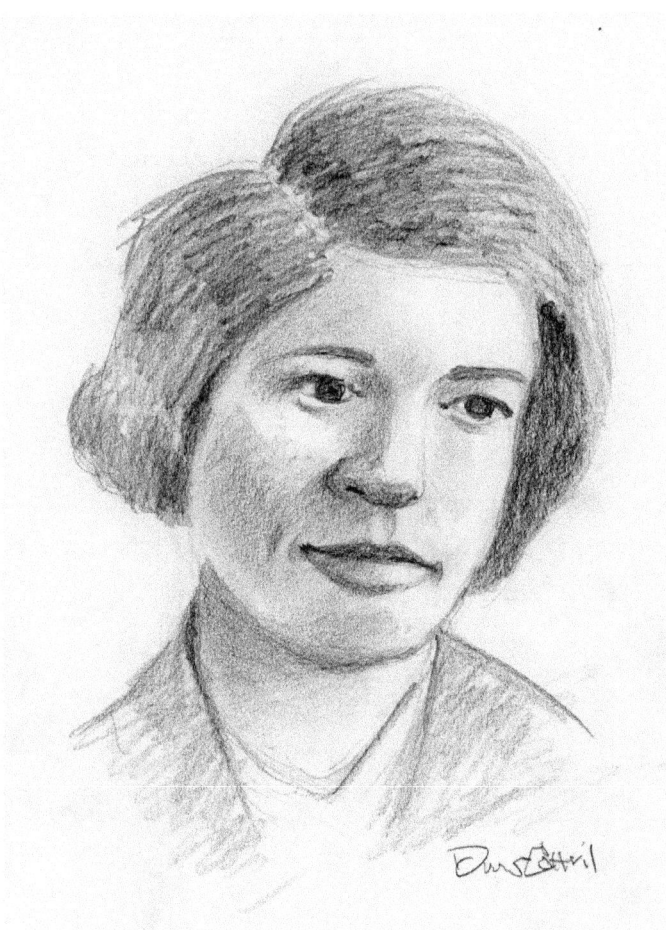

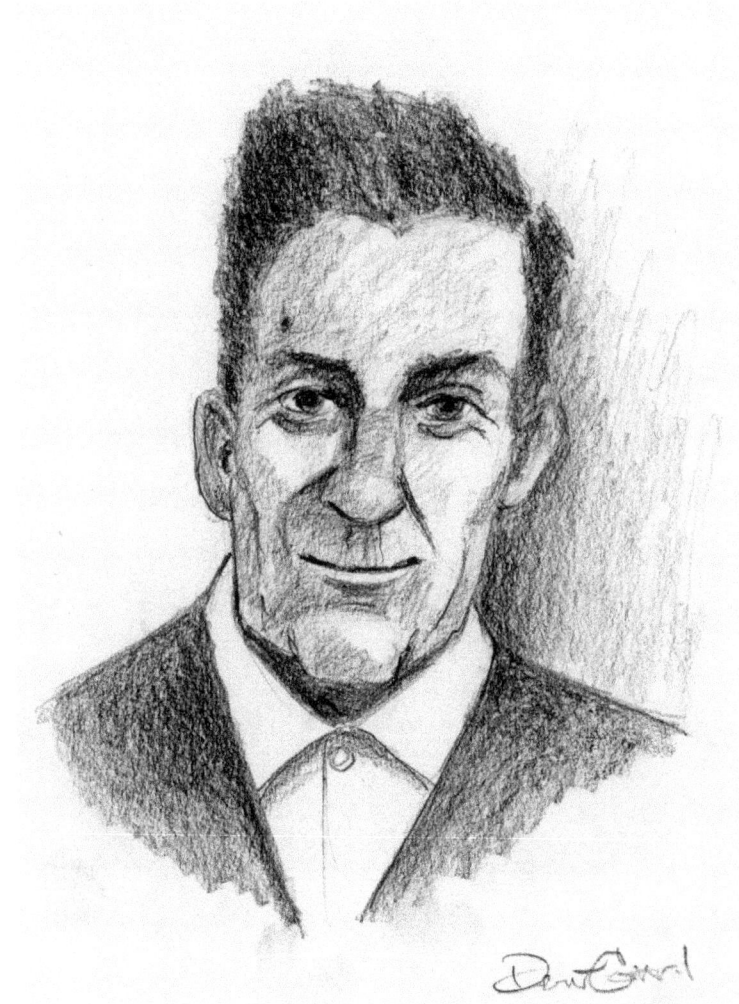

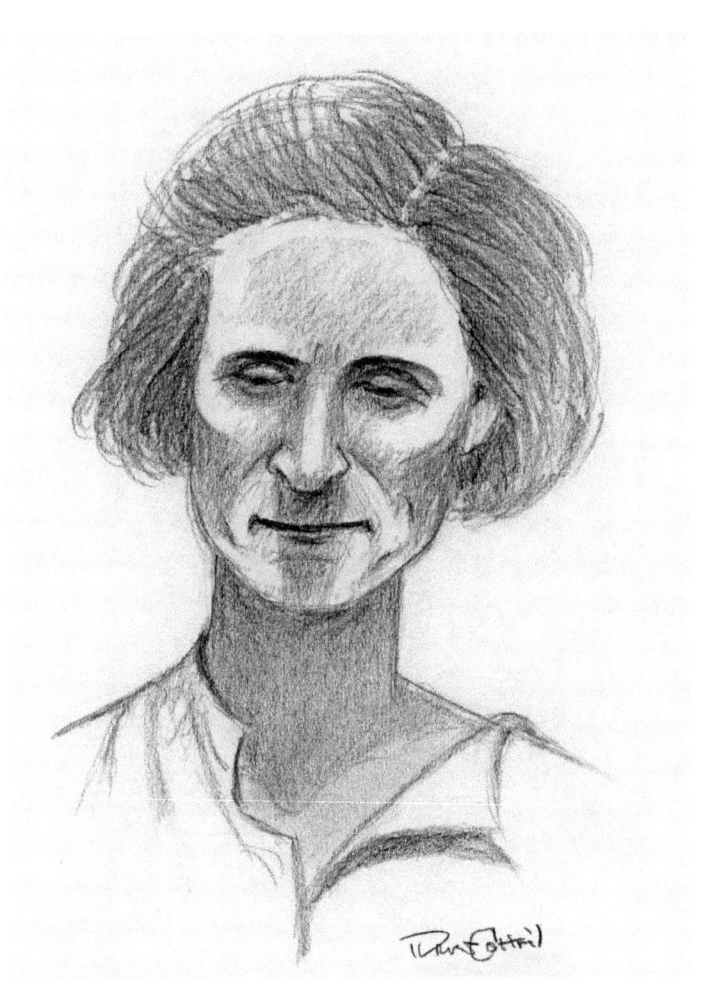

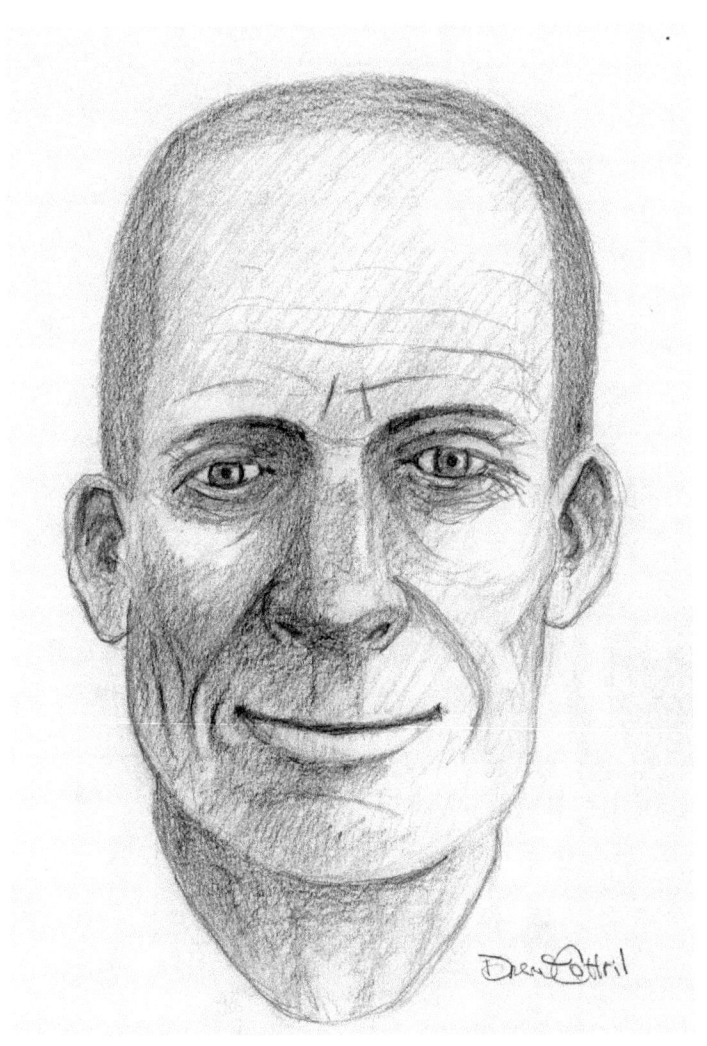

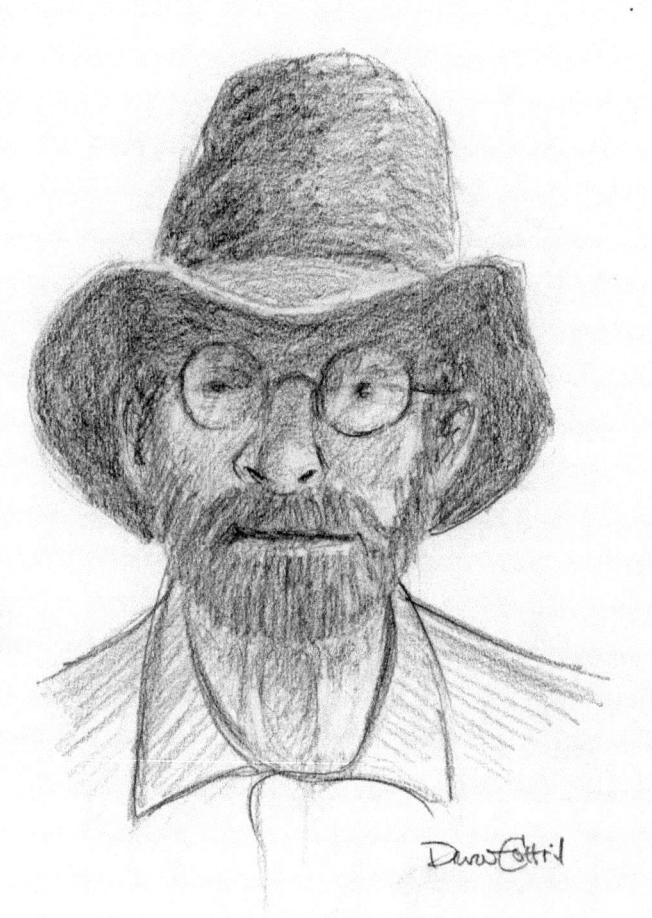

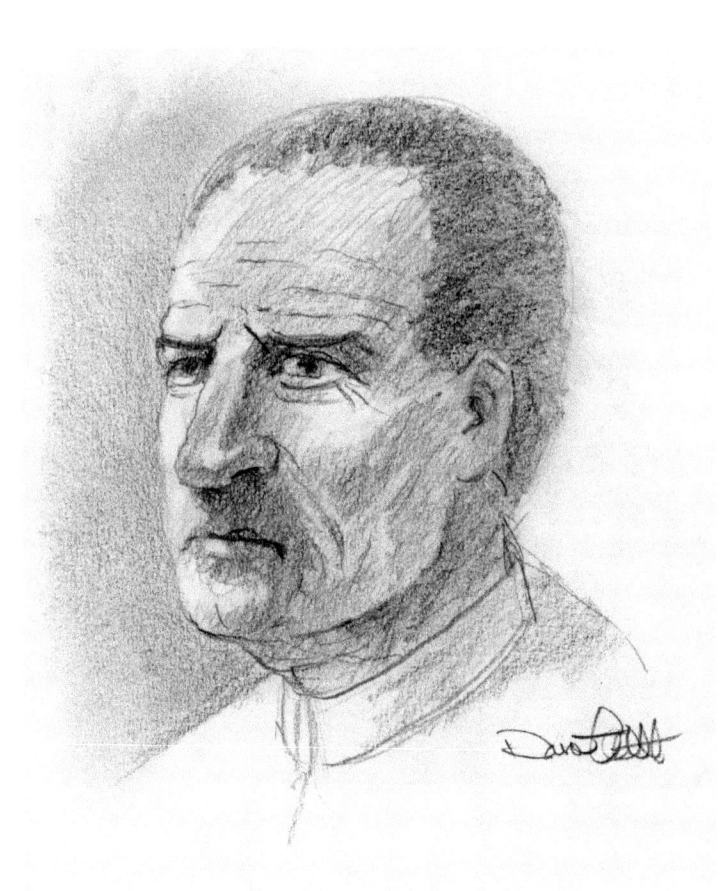

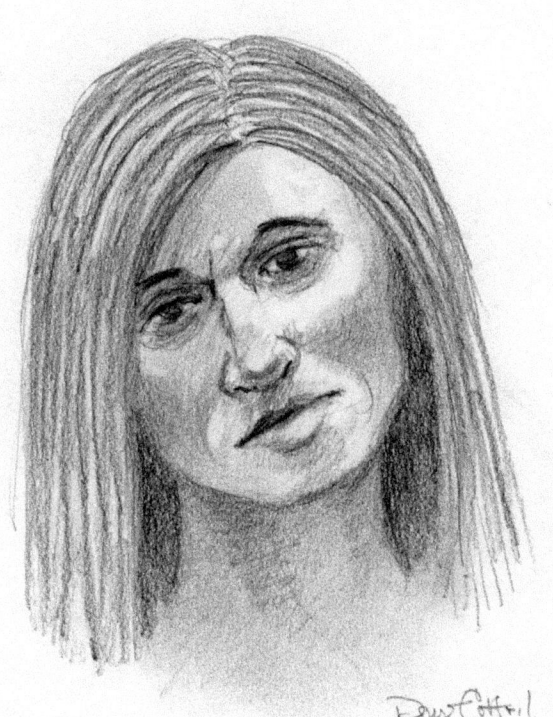

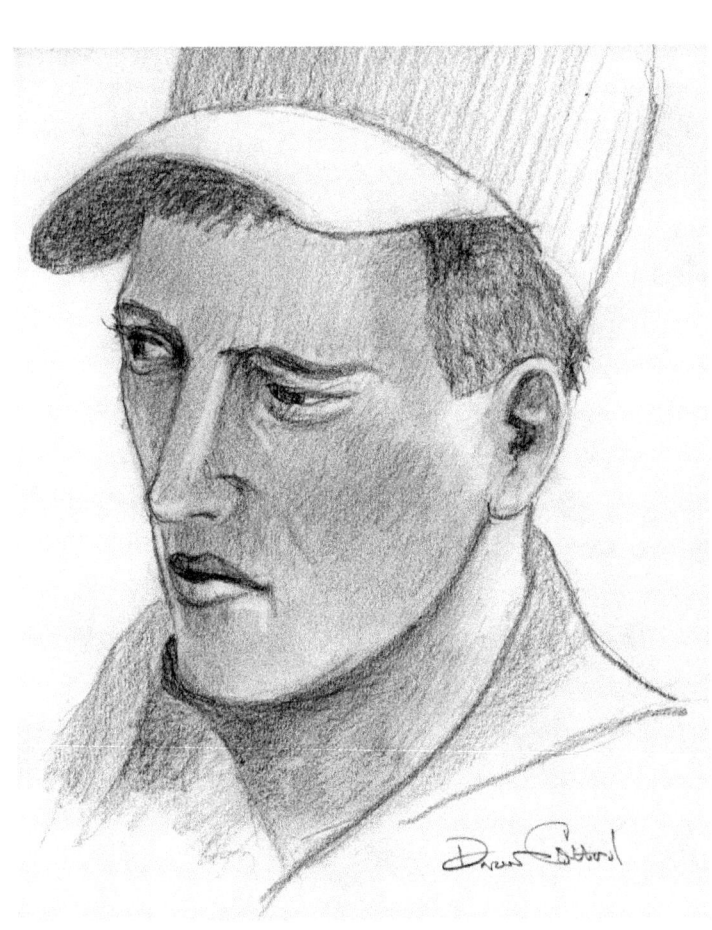

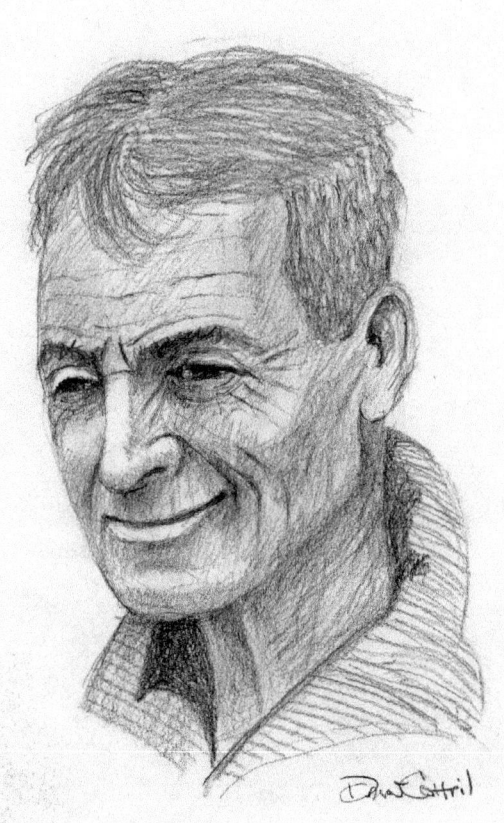

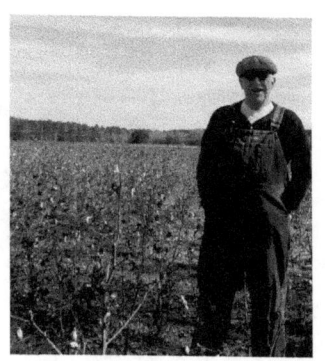

Drew Cottril lives in
Bulloch County, Georgia.
Drew teaches drawing
at the Averitt Center
for the Arts
in Statesboro, Georgia.

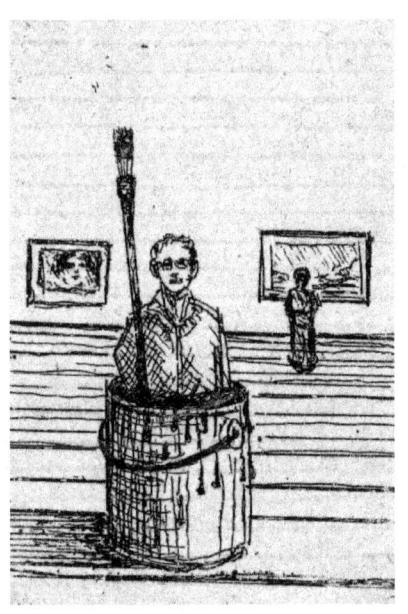